Poetry-Book One

I0171239

Phases

Of

Me

Amber Taylor

Taylor Made Day Dreams
Bringing an "imaginative break" to your day!

Phases Of Me

This is a work of realistic poetry fiction.

ISBN 978-1-948383-01-1

Taylor Made Daydreams
P.O Box 85458
Westland, MI 48185

www.TaylorMadeDaydreams.com

Dedication

I dedicate this book to my Sisters, gone from this Earth. Michelle Denise Taylor-gone so young the world did not get to see what you would become. Margrette Ann Taylor-gone in your prime, right as you were about to take the world by storm. I love you both, may you be at peace.

Author Notes

Suggested age of reading 16 and up, use your own discretion. Some poems contain adult language, themes or sexual terms. These are poems written by me in my last couple years of high school, college and beyond. These are my honest ponderings of the ups and downs of life. As well as my emotions that came with varied situations. Some poems are pure imagination as well. May you be touched, uplifted or amused by my words. Enjoy!

LIFE

LIFE

Life IS?

Tragic in its <u>longness</u>
Beautiful in its <u>sweetness</u>
Pitiful in its <u>sadness</u>
Hopeful in its <u>moments</u>
Short in its <u>happiness</u>
Meaningful in its <u>lessons</u>
Meaningless in its <u>terms</u>
Ironic in its <u>playfulness</u>
Judgmental in its <u>judgements</u>

Life...what would we do without it, what can we do with it? Life...an ongoing thing even with all the misery it brings. Life...the word of joy the word of pain. Life...so complex, yet simple in its meaning.

Life IS?

I LIVE

I Walk
I Talk
I Live

I Smile
I Laugh
I Live

I Cry
I Hurt
I Live

I Love
I Hate
I Live

I Hope
I Think
I Live

MY PEOPLE

MY PEOPLE ARE SO VARIED
IN SHAPE, SIZE AND COLOR
AND I WOULDN'T HAVE IT ANY OTHER WAY

MY PEOPLE ARE ALWAYS DIFFERENT
AS IN CREATIVE, BRILLIANT AND
IMAGINATIVE

MY PEOPLE HAVE DREAMS, HOPE, AND
ASPIRATIONS
ALL WHILE PROVIDING INSPIRATION

MY PEOPLE ARE STRONG, DEDICATED AND
STRONG WILLED
STRENGTH TO FIGHT ANOTHER DAY

MY PEOPLE HAVE SURVIVED AND WILL
SURVIVE!

MY PEOPLE WERE <u>LOVERS</u> FIRST
AND <u>FIGHTERS</u> SECOND

MY PEOPLE ARE MANY
MY PEOPLE ARE GREAT

MY PEOPLE ARE **MY PEOPLE**
AND I WOULDN'T HAVE IT ANY OTHER WAY

I Once Knew A Brother

I once knew a brother
      that could be so sweet
I once knew a brother
      who could lie and cheat

I once knew a brother
      who did so well
I once knew a brother
      that landed in jail

I once knew a brother
      who had a wife
I once knew a brother and wife
      who'd always fight

I once knew a brother
      with a bright future ahead
I once knew a brother
      who soon might be dead

This brother I know
      was brother of mine
Until he turned
      to a life of crime

A Day in My Life

A day in my life
starts out slow
6:00 in the morning
is how it goes

Slowly I rise and yawn away
the stress and rest of the other day

Up and get dressed
is how it goes
Why of why
nobody knows?

I brush my teeth
while the water runs
I comb my hair
into a sloppy bun

The time goes by
as quick as light
I rush on by
Out of sight

At school I hear
the second bell
And think to myself
my day has gone to hell

Second, third
Fourth hour too
Boring, boring
What can I do?

PHASES OF ME
AMBER TAYLOR

Fifth and sixth
are really a bitch!
I think my mind
is going to flip

To much thinking
to much work
I think, I would rather
eat brown dirt

Back on the bus
and home I go
Why of why
nobody knows?

I turn on the TV
of course to full blast
Sitting down to watch
a re-run of M*A*S*H

I start on homework
at approximately six
Of course I dose off
and dream I am rich

At around midnight
I lay my head down
To travel again
On my daily merry-go-round

What is this Hell?

The days were long and the cold temperatures *feel*
below zero
I was freezing to death, so I could not even think
My mind was going crazy, numb and dumb
I felt tired, sleepy, restless; confused as my mind could
not hold simple thoughts

What to do?
Nothing, but emptiness around me
The cold seemed never ending, so my teeth chattered
And all I could think about was home

Terrible home!
There my mind was restless, but I had freedom
Here I had to suffer in silence, fear and boredom
Not really fear but loneliness

I had two more hours to go before I could even try to
escape
Which wouldn't be that hard, I could only pray that I
did not get caught again
I knew my chances of that were nil to none
Rarely did someone escape without being recaptured
Unless...they were taken out!

Well...I didn't plan on being taken out anytime soon!

So I had to fight, hard and longer
But the cold sucked all the life out of me...every single
day!
I don't even remember how I got caught in this cruel
prison!

Day in, day out they have me toiling away
They say my sentence is at least 40 years long

No way!!

But no matter how I try and find a loop hole, I don't
succeed
I can find no legal technicality for me to get off on

Yes! Two hours have come and gone
I make my escape!

Rushing madly to the doors with the rest, I make it!
Oh the freedom feels great!
I enjoy this feeling for nearly an hour
Then the hands of time, I see them coming for me

They drag me back and once again I am cold and tired

I have four more hours before I can try and escape
again
Maybe this time I'll make it...well at least for a little
while longer
Man I just can't believe I'm back at WORK...

MY LIFE

My Life is full of wonder
  every day is a journey

My Life has many joys
  and many downfalls

My Life has many hurdles
every time I go to a store or job
  I must climb a wall

My Life is always a challenge
but because I am who I am
  I always rise to the occasion

And like my ancestors, I do not winch
or pity myself
  I just do what must be done

For **my life** is full of roses
  but along with roses come thorns

And though my ancestors lost
  a lot of blood to those thorns
It is because of them
  that in **my life** all I get are scratches

In **my life**, I drive along
a road less narrow
  with softer bumps

Adversity is a part of **my life**
Adversity has been with me since before I was born
  Passed on from generation to generation

Like the Phoenix my ancestors gave their life
  for **MY LIFE** to be reborn from the ashes

I NEED TO KNOW WHY?

I NEED TO KNOW WHY **LIFE IS SO HARD**
I NEED TO KNOW WHY **LOVE IS SO PAINFUL**
I NEED TO KNOW WHY **FRIENDSHIP IS SO BRIEF**
**I NEED TO KNOW THESE THINGS IN ORDER TO
BREATHE!**

I NEED TO KNOW WHY **SEX IS SO MEANINGLESS**
I NEED TO KNOW WHY **HEARTS ARE SO FRAGILE**
I NEED TO KNOW WHY **PAIN LASTS SO LONG**
**I NEED TO KNOW THESE THINGS IN ORDER TO
BREATHE!**

I NEED TO KNOW WHY **HATE IS SO INTENSE**
I NEED TO KNOW WHY **KNOWLEDGE IS SO DENSE**
I NEED TO KNOW WHY **PEOPLE ARE SO FAKE**
**I NEED TO KNOW THESE THINGS IN ORDER TO
BREATHE!**

I NEED TO KNOW WHY **LOVE CAN BE SO WEAK**
I NEED TO KNOW WHY **PEOPLE ARE SO CRUEL**
I NEED TO KNOW WHY **YOUR PAST CAN LINGER**
**I NEED TO KNOW THESE THINGS IN ORDER TO
BREATHE!**

These are the things I need to know why...

T-R-U-S-T

T-RUTH

R-ELIABILITY

U-NITY

S-TABILITY

T-OGETHERNESS

The Death of a Friendship

The Death of a friendship
You never see it coming
It gradually sneaks up on you
Like a snake in the grass

You think nothing of the phone calls
That were never placed
You think nothing of the stiff conversations
That takes place, on your next date

You do think it's a little odd
That you've been left out of the loop
You now have to find out your friends life
Through gossip and ruse

But never the less, friend that you are
You never give up hope
You try again to be a friend
But they just take it as a joke

You see there has been a death
You did not know
That you friend
Has dropped beside the road

They do not have
What it takes
To be a friend
Real not fake

They do not realize
That it takes two
To have a real friendship
It cannot be mended with glue

You finally see
That not all is how it should be
You see they're not capable
Of love and loyalty

But if it was a real friendship
On your part at least
Then the dying of a friendship
Is slow

After time and space
You **LET IT GO**
And soon after that
LIFE GOES ON

Choices

We all have them
We all make them
Haven't got a clue
Well you have choices just choose

Right or wrong
It all depends
On whether you go
This way or that way

Left or right
Right or left
Backwards or forward
Which way should you go

Hard Choices
Simple ones too
Just take your time
Whatever you do

Rush into it
Or let it stew
Keep the peace
Or make war
Hug they neighbor
Or their flowers destroy

Choices we all make
Shape our life from the start
It is the wise who are cautious
The young that tempt fate

Think before you speak
Or for that matter leap
Into something that's hard
That won't help your fall

For you always have Choices
It's choosing the right one
For a wrong decision can make
A life time of difference

Time

Time flies when you're having fun
Or when you're mad as hell
Or in the sun

Time can go slowly
Like the sand in an hour glass
Trickling down

It's pretty funny how time
Is at its slowest
When you need it to go fast

Sometimes you get so caught up
That time lapses
And you don't know where you are

Time is a thing you can't control
You have no power to make it
Or stop it, like a clock

If only time could be
Like a tape where you could
Pause, rewind or go forward

They say time heals all wounds but this cannot be true
Because my wound still festers
Full of puss oozing to get out

A needle can stitch it
But time can not
Only the love that broke it can mend it

Time can only prolong the pain

Graduation

Graduation
Glorious in its self
Means many things
to many people

To the parents their sad
to see their baby's go

For the rest of the family
they're glad
To see that brat
in the tilting hat

To Aunt's and Uncle's
It is pride abound
To see their nieces and nephews
walk down the aisle

To the teacher it's a time
to relax and enjoy
Glorifying in a job well done

It is a time for the coaches and counselors
to give themselves a pat on the back
For advice well given and received

It's a time when seniors
have the biggest smiles

PHASES OF ME
AMBER TAYLOR

A time to rejoice
and look back and reflect
A time to look forward
to the road ahead
A time to say your prayers
For even making it *here*

To a new beginning
that was hard fought and won

Money Woes

A universal problem
For a universal world
Even the rich once had them
They're called money woes

They're a different kind of blues
That involves finance
Having money to spend
Is what makes us grin

Money Woes
Can make you sad
Often times make you mad

They can make you depressed
Or make you regress
Either way it goes, money woes
Is by no means a joke

LIFE GOES ON

<u>Life Goes On</u>
It never stops
Not for me
And not for you

<u>Life Goes On</u>
It cannot rest
It beats us all
It's our hardest test

<u>Life Goes On</u>
Through joy and pain
It does not stop
It cannot be slain

<u>Life Goes On</u>
For me and you
Even when we are gone
LIFE...will still go on

Life As We Know It

Life as we know it
  Is harsh at best
Struggling against it
  Is the realest test

Life as we know it
  Can also be sweet
Filled with promises
  We hope to keep

In our hour of need
  When life is at its lowest
Many rise to the occasion
  But many will also fall

Battle the forces of evil
  Live life at its fullest
Let troubles not concern us so deep
  To keep our sanity and peace

You must compete in life's game
  I just hope you win
Because many have been trampled
  Running Life's race

Life as we know it, can bring great joy
Life as we know it, sometimes treats us as its toy

Peace

A little quiet word
But oh so very hard to obtain

Peace
You can say it on a whisper
Or a shout

Peace a thing of the past
And maybe of the future

Peace a thing to be embraced at all costs
If it ever should come across your path

Peace embodies quiet and stillness all around

LOVE

Young, Sad & Blue

I used to be young, sad and blue
because we were through

I use to be young
but that is no more
Through my pain
I have become old

I used to love you
now I don't

After I lost your love
I became sad
Filled with despair

I hated the world
and did not care
After I regained my sanity
and realized I had not loved you for a while

I became blue
mellow and dramatic
Looking this time for real love

My heart felt empty
Depressed and blue

Yes, I was once too
Young, Sad & Blue

Though I am over the Death-I still Grieve

I sigh

Though I am over the Death of my love
I still grieve

I grieve for the time
  shared and wasted
I grieve for the laughter
  and tears released

Though I love him no more
  and I am fine with that
But I grieve for the love it self

It was a precious thing
A special thing
A fragile thing
Now…a non-existent thing

I grieve for the love
  that brought a smile to my lips
I grieve for my lips
  that now do not smile

I grieve for the love
  that once filled my heart
Now I grieve for an ache in my heart
  that simply will not stop

I grieve for my happiness
 that was so bright
I grieve for this pain
 that took away my light

Though I do not grieve
 for the boy who lost my love
I do grieve
 because he lost it

Though I do not grieve
 for what he tried to give
I do grieve
 for what he could not give

I remember the touches
The hugs
The kisses

I grieve for them now
 for they are now missing

I grieve for my heart
 that beated to fast
I grieve for my heart
 that now won't move at all

I grieve for my soul
 that had found its mate
I grieve for my soul
 that now feels hate

I grieve for my mind
   that would not accept
I grieve for my mind
   that did not detect

I grieve for my mind
   when my love died

So though I am over the death
I still grieve

I sigh

My Spanish Lover

My Spanish lover
was sweet and kind
Whenever I had doubts
he eased them out my mind

He wined and dined me
and gave me gifts
I felt like a princess
with each and every kiss

He bought me flowers
from far and beyond
He showed me kindness
which had never been done

He opened my eyes
to a whole new world
And made me see
that happiness could…still be for me

For this I owe him many thanks!
And it is quite evident that he has Gods grace
I hope he knows he has mine too,
for I will never forget the things

My Spanish Lover would do

All That You Could Be

I was wondering along
this endless road
Hoping, seeking
a Savior for me

Suddenly you appeared
clear out the blue
Telling me words I longed to hear
and so for that I pushed away my fears

Part of me knew, it would not last
Part of me resisted you being a fad
I wanted you to be my Savior, Alex Savior to me
But deep in my heart, I knew it could not be

I wanted you to be Alex
Savior to me
But all that you could be
was my Spanish lover to me

Love

Love
Like all things
Comes and goes
Like summer's spring

Washed away like
Sumer's tide
Still some think
That love abides

Star-crossed lovers
Would like to think
That loves binds the heart
In just one week

Love can seem so very true
But in a day can be so through
I wish oh wish
That it could last

Instead it goes
Into my past
There are *some* loves
That stay and last

But to this day
I've never found
That lasting love
To be around

On a Winter Night

On a Winter Night
With the wind howling
And the snow banging on the door
We made love

On the plush floor rug
In front of the flames of our passion
We joined

By the shadow of the candles
I watched our bodies move
In the amber light
And I didn't feel the chill at all

Our concerns and reality flew away
On the fierce wind
While our emotions and bodies
Heated up like the fire

On that winter night
We did not think
About the morning to come
Or obligations

For on a winter night
I was the happiest
I had ever been in my life

But with the wind in my ears
And fire in my limbs
I forgot that even winter nights
Come to an end

My Valentine

My Valentine
So dear so sweet so true
Loves me like the brightest light

He gives me gifts and treats me right
So that at night we do not fight
Instead we love in candle light

I love him so, as much as my might
He loves me back, as much as his sight

He gives me time
I give him mine
We drink some wine
And then we dine

Cause all year round
He's my Valentine.

Real Love

Real Love
What does it mean?
Is it just a term
Or all a dream

Real love, if you've ever had it
Never goes away
Real Love is not skin deep
But soul deep

Real love brings the sweetest joy
Real love brings the deepest pain
To real love nothing can compare
But to loss it, is the saddest despair

Real love is the reddest rose that blooms
Real love is the sweetest perfume

Real love turns a seer into a blind man
A healthy man into a cripple
But the waves of love, work both ways
Real love can make a blind man see
Make the weak strong, make right a wrong

Real love is funny in many ways
It can happen in a second
Or over many days

The strength of real love could part the sea
The intensity of real love could fight a war
The emotions that real love creates
Are infinite in number

Real love is a mask
That can never be shed
Many faces can be painted over it
But with time the paint will wear and tare

Real love will endure through time and space
Real love is the judge, jury and case
Real love has no equal when it hates
Real love is pure in heart, if sometimes not in soul

Real love grows but can also be diminished
Real love flows much like a winding river

Real love is different than obsession or lust
Real love is a candle that never goes out
Real love is a fire whose flames never fade

Real love will last eternally
Forever and a day

My Lost Love

My lost love
Was good while it lasted
Though it seems it only
Lasted a millisecond
In my life

My lost love
Was hell for me
To go through so much
You cannot, would not perceive

So hellish the devil
Turned his head
And Jesus wept

My lost love
I hope is never found
My lost love however
Will always be around

In the dark cold
Recesses of my mind
Will forever live
The memories
Of my lost love

Homie Lover Friend

My homie lover friend is what you are to me

You're my homie cause we can kick it, anytime anywhere

You're my friend because you make me laugh and listen and try to care

You're my lover cause I want you so, just in case you did not know

I fiend for you when I close my eyes
Thoughts of you in my head can make me high

As a homie lover friend, you're perfect for me
As anything else, we'll have to wait and see

Angst

My Soul

My Soul

A cold lonely thing
A transparent thing
A battered thing
A fragile thing

My Soul
Which once was strong
   and now is weak

My soul
Once full of hope
   now leaks despair

My Soul

A tired thing
A rejected thing
A lost thing
A imaginary thing

My Soul

Nothing Even Matters No More...

The Sun went down
And for a moment
I thought I'd die
Cause nothing even matters no more...

I used to be young, sad & blue
Now I'm old, happy & true
I know who I am, I know what I want
Cause nothing even matters no more...

Out went my heart
And in came the cold
So confused, I knew not what to do
Cause nothing even matters no more...

I'm content now
Sure of *myself*
I still have a journey to go
Cause nothing even matters no more...

This life so full of surprises
Some *good* and some *bad*
Some *joyful* and some *sad*
Cause nothing even matters no more...

My *dreams* once so far way
Seem *closer* day by day
All I need is time and space
Cause nothing even matters no more...

My heart beats now
A little warmer than before
But still my mind just really doesn't know
Cause nothing even matters no more...

I've been through *better* times
I've been through *worse*
It's all so irrelevant
Cause nothing even matter no more...

I AM DONE

I AM DONE...with people who take my love and run

I AM DONE...with "friends" who don't care for me, as much as I care for them

I AM DONE...with fakes, liars and cheats

I AM DONE...with "sorry" "I didn't mean" and "it's not my fault"

I AM DONE...with people who abuse and use my compassion
DAMN IT!!!

I AM DONE...so don't come up to me asking "why" or "what did I do"?

Never again will I give to you my friendship and love...for **I AM DONE**

The Dying of a Heart

The dying of a heart
  is usually very slow
It takes many times of abuse
  to stop it's loving flow
From flowing through the veins of life

When all hope leaves and all that's left is grief
When sorrow is not enough
  and despair quietly creeps

Creeps up on you
  at the oddest of times
Loosening your grip
  on reality and sanity

And is not sanity
  our dearest life line?
Without we are a shell of a person
  without a thing inside

When you feel nothing
  not pain, not grief, not anger
When your soul is empty
  and you feel you have nothing else to loose

When you feel you've felt the pain as bad as it can get
When you feel you've cried the grief forever and a day
When you feel the last drop of hope finally slip away
Then your heart has died a dying hearts death

Now that it's dead you may rest in peace
Never to worry about a heart and all its grief

ALEX

If life was just a figment of our imagination…everything
would be all right

Where is my Alex?
Where are you in my time of need?
Please be my Savior, do not leave me in my deepest hour

For without you
I shall parish at the waste side
No breath shall leave my body
No blood shall pump in my veins
For nothing else will be my Savior

Since I made the *bad choice*
I've been walking on the edge
I'll ask only once for you…are my last hope

Please save me from destruction, which I have brought upon
myself
But I ask you now
Please deliver me from my everlasting grief

There's not an hour that goes by that I am not suffering
I ask you now to help me Alex
for I don't think I'll have the strength to ask again

The black shadow of death creeps upon me
and I hold it off only for you!
But my grip is slipping every day
So if you are coming hurry for there is no time left
and no hope in my soul

Death

When in the valley of death, hang thy head low
But do not look away from death
For death will come whether you look it in the face or
not

Death will come when you are asleep
Death can come when you are at peace
There are lucky few who death comes to in torture

Death also comes in times of despair
Death can be a tidal wave that swallows all in its path
Death can be painless or very hard for those who fight it
or hide from it

People are afraid of death but not I
For there is nothing to fear but fear itself

For if you live your life right to begin with, there is no
need to fear it in the end
Have no regrets for what you do
Make good choices and your death will be uneventful
too

Some embrace death welcoming it into their home
Feeding it tea and cake

Death is not just for the old, poor and sick
Death has its choice of all, and rightly takes its pick
Some of us are high and some of us are low
But in the end we all grow mold and decay

Life is like a candle and Death is like the wind
Life comes in many forms straw, wood and brick
And Death like the big bad wolf will blow them
down...even the brick after awhile

Death is as quick as lighting
And as smart as a fox
Or slow as a turtle
And dumb as an ox

Death is impartial
Not biased at all
It has no preferences against black and white
Like we so often do

So in the end, Death will kill us all
And not care a fig about me or you

I Hate

I Hate
the hate
that made me hate

The hate
the anger
is it really my fate?

This hate
so deep
it makes me weep

I hate
the world
in all its grief

I hate
the power
I cannot see

The power
that does
these things to me

I hate
my self
for feeling this way

I hate
the hate
that made me hate

I'm Tired of This Game

I'm so damn tired of this game
I really am
Of playing these games
every damn day

Bitches hoes sluts too
All up in mine
I ain't got the time

Stepping on my toes
you dingy ass hoes
You betta get back
before you get jacked

And for that punk ass nigga
you really ain't shit
I won't play your game
so now your pissed

Trying play all smooth
With those fucking hoes
If you don't come correct
Then push eject

See ya!
Bye Bye!
Three strikes
you're out!

You already got two
so what's that all about?

I'm to old to play games
Like back in the day
I need more than you can give
and that's for real

I might want your body
but that's about it
With an attitude like yours
who gives a shit!

So take your weak ass on
and play them games
With those mangy tricks
that suck your dick

To all the girls
good luck to you
You bitches can have him
cause I'm totally through

Jealous

How can I be jealous
of the ones I call my friends
They have something I don't
something I want

Something I see
but cannot touch
It's only half mine
so how can I whine?

The sound of them laughing
The sight of them playing
Makes me so sad
For I have the same craving

Tell me what should I do
You really can't say
Unless you've been jealous too

Suicide

A sinister word
But harmless in itself
Death I do not embrace
But peace of mind I do

Release is what I crave
Not a duggin fresh grave
I need to go to another place
And suicide is my ride

You see I've realized that I'm to tipsy to drive

I want off of this ride
I was told "in due time"
But I'm paranoid
And cannot wait

I feel if I don't get off now
I'll Die

So I jump
I soar, I fly
For once I feel free
Then with a thud...I die

My Frozen Smile

I walk along a lonely road
No one to turn to, nowhere to go
I kick a rock and throw a stick
But no one's there to see me pitch
Don't be sad cause I'm not mad
Cause on my face is a frozen smile

Sometimes as I walk along this road
I meet a couple friends or foes

When I come upon a friend, with all their many woes
My frozen smile lights up their face
And along the road they go
But when I come upon a foe
My frozen smile is flashed also

Just like my smile
My feelings are froze inside

If people just knew what I really felt
Then maybe my frozen smile would melt
Melt into anger, joy or fear

Anything to make me feel alive...because I'm dead
inside
My frozen smile is a mask

To hide my deepest thoughts

GOD

Fake Followers

Dear Lord,
Did you know
that you have
FAKE FOLLOWERS?

> Well I did
> You have scores of them
> These people called FAKE FOLLOWERS
> Let me point them out to you

You say be humble
For conceit is not good
But they must buy brand names
Then hair and nails

> They drink three
> Or four days in a row
> Then they go to church
> And sit in the front pew

They fornicate at will
With a smile on their face
And then they ask for forgiveness
And *your* loving grace

> Those who preach
> Love and compassion for all
> Then turn around
> And talk about all

To show compassion
This is what they do
They turn their heads
And spit on Jews

PHASES OF ME
AMBER TAYLOR

These FAKE FOLLOWERS
Are many and wide
I just don't know
Why they can't be honest inside

No one is perfect
We all know this
So, don't act like you're holy
And then throw fits

Don't say that you're saved
And then act *extra* wild
Just admit that you're average
And then go that extra mile

Just because you can quote
Verse by verse
Doesn't mean
That the rest of us are cursed

Do you know how easy it is
To memorize text?
But if you don't follow it
Why even go to church?

Practice what you preach
Is all I ask
Because I know I don't like dealing with fakes and neither
do you
So what makes you think that the Lord wants to?

Child of God Am I

Child of God am I
If nothing else I am this
Just because I do not pray
Five times a Day
Does not mean <u>my love is less</u>

Child of God am I
If nothing else I am this
Just because I do not agree with
Every word in the book
Does not mean <u>my faith is less</u>

Child of God am I
If nothing else I am this
Just because I practice
In a different way
Does not mean <u>my belief is less</u>

Child of God am I
If nothing else I am this
Just because I am not
Your prefect image
Does not mean <u>my image is less</u>

We are all God's children
For child of God I am
Nothing more, nothing less
Child of God I am
If nothing else I am this

NATURE

Weather

The weather is cold
The weather is hot
The weather is sunny
Not today it's not

The weather is windy
The weather is dry
Today will be a flood
Tomorrow will be a drought

The weather is chilly
The weather is warm
The weather is rainy
The weather is clear

The weather is misty
In that far field

For just two days
I would like to see
The weather alike
Just for me

Dedicated to Michigan's ever changing weather

Tears of the Moon

The color is silver…what else could they be, as they
trail through space
They create glittery stardust…what a waste, of the
great creation

Their taste is that of despair, of the blackest deepest pits
For tears of the moon are tragic, deep felt & meant

When the moon feels such cold desolate agony
The universe dims, blocked from happiness within

The day the moon wept
Every atom cried

Even so, some particles stretched and smiled
The moon can only light up the world, never darken it,
they sang

So along with the ache of pain
Hope and love trail across the galaxy with every stream

Though tears of the moon should never be shed, there
is still not a number great enough to douse the moons
effervescent glow

PETS

The Walnut Tree

As I sit upon this window sill
I think of you

I think about you
Out beyond the window pane
Playing in the grass

I see you climb the walnut tree
Up and up you go
Chasing a caterpillar as it grows

I see myself
Climbing up
To help you climb back down

I see us laying beneath this window
You laying in my lap
As we snuggle up
To get a sun warmed nap

I can see you running after a bird
And me running after you
Yelling "you naughty kitten don't eat that bird"
Even while you chewed

I can see you sitting in the bushes
In your later years
Pretending you didn't hear me
Until the can opener buzzed

PHASES OF ME
AMBER TAYLOR

In my mind
I see all these things

But in reality
All I see
Is you...
Buried beneath the Walnut Tree

**Dedicated to Tommy with Love
Baby Boy #1**

Angel...Angel Of Mine

A need out the blue...drew me to you
It was confusing at the time, since I was content and felt
just fine
But something inside me pushed to search for your
kind

I'll never be able to say...what drew me just to *you*
But holding you sealed the deal
And our new life's journey began anew

You were tenacious from the start!
Your personality bigger than you!
Feisty and precocious, adventurous too!

Little did I know your purpose would soon be revealed
For tragedy soon struck my life, hard enough to kill
A blow so deep to me, I thought I could not live

But through it all, big and small, you were there right
by my side
With me every night when my pillow caught my tears
With me every time I yelled "this is to much! I just can't
deal!"

It was then I realized, why I had felt such intense need
for you
You were to be my life line, when I drifted out, my
everlasting crutch
Why I named you *Angel*, when you were anything but
such

Sometimes I see "that spirit" in the sparkle of your eyes
As the years fly by you comfort me still, especially
when I cry
Or when I'm sick or lonely you stay close by my side

You helped to fill the void I've felt since that day of
dark dismay
You were an Angel sent, from up above, to help me
through the gray
I hope I've given you, at least *half* back, of what you've
given me

**Dedicated with Love to Angel on your 10th year of
sharing your life with me**

PHASES OF ME
AMBER TAYLOR

www.ingramcontent.com/pod-product-compliance
Lightning Source LLC
Chambersburg PA
CBHW060701030426
42337CB00017B/2713